#
TOFU GOES WEST

**Recipes by Gary Landgrebe**

**Illustrations by Seraphina Landgrebe**

**Introduction by Sharon Elliot**

fresh press

this book is dedicated
　　　　to the one in all
　　　　　　　who waits so patiently
　　　　　　　　　　for all to be at one
　　　　　　　　　　　　　with all that is

A special thanks goes out to Seraphina for much love and light along with all her help; to Junauro and Oradona for patience and a willingness to change; and to Anna, Connie, Christmas, Gene, Marie, and Theresa for the energy and love they gave.

Book Design by Sandy Haight

Published by Fresh Press
　　　　3712  Ortega Court
　　　　Palo Alto, California  94303

Library of Congress Number: 78-67462
ISBN: O-9601398-2-6

First Edition: December 1978
Sixth Printing: 1986

# TOFU GOES WEST

# CONTENTS

# AUTHOR'S PREFACE

In looking back over these recipes, I remember the many superlatives used to describe them, things like incredible, fantastic and super. This is a true reflection of my enthusiasm for what has happened. For awhile we were trying two or three recipes a day. It was always rewarding to have them turn out so remarkably different. People would say, "When you get done with this book, you'll never want to see that stuff again." The result has been quite the contrary. I am even more impressed with the versatility and adaptability of tofu today than I could ever have been before. It offers so many possibilities that I cannot help being thankful for having had the chance to work so closely with it.

*Gary Landgrebe*

# INTRODUCTION

Until a few years ago, I'd never heard of tofu. I remember the first time I saw it in the vegetable section at the market. The produce man told me it was made from soy beans, had almost no flavor, and was used in oriental dishes. He said he stocked it in the produce section because it was often used with vegetables and needed to be constantly refrigerated.

Intrigued by this strange, water-bathed food, I arranged to visit a small family run "tofu factory" where I could actually see tofu being made. The process looked quite simple – similar to cheese making. The family making the tofu was very enthusiastic. They called tofu "meat without the bone", and told me that people in the Orient had been eating it for centuries as one of their main protein staples.

The more I found out about tofu, the more impressed I became. It is low in calories, high in good quality protein and rich in both calcium and iron.* I introduced it to my family in a few salad dressings, soups, and dinner loaves — no objections, but no raves either. I was getting frustrated because I couldn't find many ways to use tofu in my everyday cooking.

*See the appendix for further details.

Shortly after the publication of my BUSY PEOPLE'S FAST FOODBOOK, I received Gary Landgrebe's TOFU GOES WEST manuscript in the mail. I began to try his recipes. I was sold right away! My family was a bit wary at first — "This couldn't have tofu in it, it tastes so good" ... or "Whoever heard of tofu in bread. Can I have another piece?" It wasn't long before they each had several favorite tofu dishes.

Gary has chosen a food just right for our times — low in calories, high in nutrients, inexpensive, and ecologically positive in all respects. He has combined it with well known, widely enjoyed ingredients to create tasty, American-style dishes. His recipes are easy to follow and offer great variety: delicate (Mushroom Crepes) to spicy (Chili Con Tofu), crispy (Tofu Croutons) to silky smooth (Almond Creme Pie). Even the hard-to-please eater will find delights in TOFU GOES WEST.

I've noted below some information about tofu that Gary and I want to share with you. For more detailed information we refer you to THE BOOK OF TOFU.*

## TOFU

The ingredient listing on a typical package of tofu specifies water, soybeans, and usually either nigari or calcium sulfate (the solidifiers used to coagulate the tofu). Tofu's ingredient listing would have read the same thousands of years ago for today's tofu is made by an age-old process. Soybeans are soaked for several hours and then puréed with water. The purée is brought to a boil

*Shurtleff, William, and Aoyagi, Akiko, THE BOOK OF TOFU, Autumn Press, U.S.A., 1975.

in a large pot and then strained through a cloth. The crude fibers of the soy bean are caught in the cloth and discarded. The remaining liquid, called soy milk, is returned to the pot. After it has simmered for a few minutes a small amount of solidifier is added. This causes the milk to separate into curds (tofu!) and whey. The curds are ladled into tofu molds, pressed into the familiar shape, and chilled. Through this simple process the highly nutritious essence of the soy bean becomes available to our bodies in a form that can be easily utilized.

There are many different varieties of tofu on the market today: deep fried, grilled, and fermented, to name a few. The tofu called for in TOFU GOES WEST, however, is always the fresh, creamy white kind. There are two basic types of this kind of tofu: the softer Chinese (set with calcium sulfate, the purified form of gypsum) and the harder Japanese (set with nigari, a natural by-product of salt making.) Either of these may be used successfully in TOFU GOES WEST recipes.

## BUYING TOFU

The flavor and texture of tofu are determined by its freshness and the type of solidifier used. When buying tofu, check the date on the package; it usually indicates the date before which the tofu should be used. Ask your grocer to be sure. The fresher the tofu, the sweeter and lighter its flavor. As tofu ages it develops a distinctive tang. This may add character to a main dish, but for breads and desserts use only the freshest tofu.

## STORING TOFU

Tofu must be covered with water and refrigerated to stay fresh. It can be kept unopened in its original package for 7 – 10 days. Once opened, however, the tofu should be transferred to another covered container, rinsed well, and covered with fresh water. The water should be changed daily.

If you have more tofu on hand than you can use within the recommended time, freeze it!

## FROZEN TOFU

Tofu may be frozen in its original container just as it comes from the store. After it has been in the freezer for a week, its texture changes from soft and custard-like to spongy. In this state it can be crumbled or sliced and used as a substitute for ground meats or pasta.

Before frozen tofu is used, it should be thoroughly thawed (but not left indefinitely at room temperature), drained of all liquid, rinsed and squeezed dry. When frozen tofu is called for in TOFU GOES WEST recipes, it is listed in terms of its weight before freezing.

## TOFU AS A PROTEIN SOURCE

Four ounces of fresh tofu contain 8.8 grams of high quality protein, comparable to chicken or steak in its usefulness to the body. Tofu's protein potential can be further enhanced if it is

10

served with milk, eggs, cheese, grains (such as millet or wheat, especially wheat bran, oats, and rice), cornmeal, sesame or sunflower seeds, or vegetables such as spinach and corn. All the recipes in TOFU GOES WEST are examples of tasty, simple ways to combine these foods with tofu to achieve a protein usability higher than that found in most other foods.

## TOFU AS A DIET FOOD

Tofu is an ideal food for weight watchers. An eight ounce serving contains only 147 – 164 calories, but provides over one-fourth of the suggested daily protein allowance for an adult male, as well as an abundance of other vitamins and minerals.*

## TOFU AND DIGESTIBILITY

Since tofu is made from soy beans you might wonder about its digestibility. You'll be happy to know that the hard to digest crude fibers and water soluble carbohydrates found in soy beans are automatically removed during the tofu-making process. Tofu is an excellent food for babies, surgical recuperees, and other people with special digestive needs.

*Sharon Elliot*

*See the appendix for further details.

# TOFU MAIN DISHES

# SPAGHETTI SAUCE

Sauté for about 5 minutes
>    1 LARGE ONION, CHOPPED
>    4 LARGE CLOVES GARLIC, MINCED

In

>    2 TBS. OLIVE OIL

Add

>    1 LB. TOFU, MASHED WELL WITH A FORK
>    1 CAN (15 OZ.) TOMATO SAUCE
>    1 CAN (28 OZ.) TOMATOES
>    1 BAY LEAF
>    1½ TSP. ITALIAN SEASONING OR ½ TSP. <u>EACH</u>
>       OREGANO, BASIL AND THYME
>    ¼ TSP. PEPPER
>    1 TBS. BEEF FLAVORED BOUILLON
>    ½ – 1 CUP SLICED MUSHROOMS

Bring to a boil, reduce heat and simmer, covered, for 30 minutes.
Stir frequently.
Makes 2 quarts.

# ASIAN DELIGHT

Sauté for about 3 minutes
>1 LARGE ONION, THINLY SLICED
>2 CLOVES GARLIC, MINCED

In
>3 TBS. OIL (PEANUT OR SESAME, PREFERABLY)

Add
>1 CUP WATER
>3 TBS. SOY SAUCE
>1 TBS. BEEF FLAVORED BOUILLON
>1 TBS. + 1 TSP. LIGHT MOLASSES
>2 TBS. PEANUT BUTTER
>¼ TSP. CARDAMON
>⅛ TSP. NUTMEG
>¼ CUP RAISINS
>¼ CUP CASHEW PIECES, LIGHTLY TOASTED

Stir until the peanut butter is well blended.

Add
>1 LB. TOFU, DICED IN ¼" CUBES
>2 MEDIUM BANANAS, SLICED IN HALF
>  LENGTHWISE AND THEN IN ½" PIECES.

Simmer for 5 minutes, stirring frequently.

Serves 4 – 5. Good with millet* or rice.

*See page 45.

# TOFU
# CHEESE SAUCE

Mix in a blender until smooth
    ½ CUP MILK
    12 OZ. TOFU
    ½ TSP. SALT
    ½ TSP. DRY MUSTARD
    ¼ TSP. PAPRIKA
    FRESH GROUND PEPPER
      OR A FEW GRAINS CAYENNE

Melt in a large sauce pan
    1 TBS. BUTTER

Pour the tofu mixture into the pan.
Add
    1½ CUPS GRATED CHEDDAR
      CHEESE
    1 TBS. GRATED PARMESAN CHEESE

Stir until the cheese has melted and the
mixture is bubbly.

# TOFU RAREBIT

Mix in a blender until smooth
>1 CAN (15 OZ.) TOMATO SAUCE
>1 LB. TOFU
>1 TSP. DRY MUSTARD
>1 TSP. WORCESTERSHIRE SAUCE
>½ TSP. SALT
>¼ TSP. PAPRIKA
>A BIT OF FRESH GROUND PEPPER OR CAYENNE

Warm in a heavy skillet over medium heat
>1 TBS. OIL

Pour the tofu mixture into the skillet.
Add
>2 – 3 CUPS GRATED AGED CHEESE

Stir until the cheese has melted and the mixture is bubbly.
Ladle over toast or crackers.
Serves 4.

# CANNELLONI

Cook and drain
> 8 MANICOTTI SHELLS

Mix well in a large bowl
> 1 LB. TOFU, MASHED WELL WITH A FORK
> 1 EGG, LIGHTLY BEATEN
> 1½ TSP. PARSLEY
> ½ TSP. NUTMEG
> ½ TSP. BASIL
> ½ TSP. SALT
> ¼ TSP. PEPPER
> ¼ CUP GRATED PARMESAN CHEESE
> 1 CUP GRATED CHEDDAR CHEESE

Fill the manicotti shells with the tofu mixture.
Lay the manicotti down the center of an oiled 9" x 13" baking dish.

Cover with
> 1 CAN (15 OZ.) ITALIAN-STYLE TOMATO SAUCE
> (MIXED WITH ANY REMAINING STUFFING).

Sprinkle with
> GRATED PARMESAN CHEESE

Bake at 350° for 30 minutes.
Serves 4.

# MUSHROOM SKILLET BAKE

Sauté in a large oven-proof skillet over medium heat
    1 MEDIUM ONION, CHOPPED

In

    2 – 3 TBS. OIL

Add and sauté for 3 minutes more
    4 CUPS SLICED MUSHROOMS (TIGHTLY PACKED)
Remove from heat.

Stir in
    12 OZ. TOFU, MASHED WELL WITH A FORK
    ½ CUP MILK
    3 EGGS, LIGHTLY BEATEN
    1 TSP. SALT
    ¼ TSP. PEPPER
    ¼ TSP. GARLIC POWDER
    1 CUP GRATED CHEDDAR OR SWISS CHEESE

Bake at 350° for 30 – 35 minutes.
Serves 4 – 5.

# MEXICAN CHEESE PIE

**THE CRUST** (OPTIONAL)

Prepare your favorite unsweetened, single, 10" crust.
Prick well with a fork.
Bake at 450° for 7 minutes.

**THE FILLING**

Mix in a blender until smooth
      1½ LBS. TOFU
      1 CUP BUTTERMILK
      1 CAN (6 OZ.) TOMATO PASTE
      1 TBS. HONEY
      2 EGGS
      1¼ TSP. SALT
      ½ – ¾ TSP. CUMIN (TO TASTE)
      ¼ TSP. PAPRIKA
      ¼ TSP. CORIANDER
      ¼ TSP. CAYENNE
      2 TBS. FLOUR
Pour into a large bowl.

Continued

Stir in
> 2 TBS. DEHYDRATED ONION FLAKES
> 1½ CUPS GRATED CHEDDAR CHEESE
> ¼ CUP GRATED PARMESAN CHEESE
> 2 CUPS GRATED MONTEREY JACK CHEESE
> 1 CAN (4½ OZ.) CHOPPED BLACK OLIVES

Turn into the prepared crust or a 10" baking dish.
Bake at 325° for 1 hour.
Let stand for 15 minutes before serving.
Serves 6 – 8.

# TOFU CHILI CHEESE SQUARES

Mix in a blender until smooth
>6 EGGS
>1½ LBS. TOFU
>1½ TSP. SALT

Turn into a large bowl.
Stir in
>2 LBS. CHEDDAR CHEESE, GRATED
>2 CANS (4 OZ. EACH) CHOPPED GREEN CHILIS

Spread evenly in an oiled 9" x 13" pan.
Sprinkle with
>GRATED PARMESAN CHEESE

Dust with
>PAPRIKA

Bake at 350° for 30 – 35 minutes.
Serves 10 – 12 as a main dish, or makes about 100 appetizers.

# ITALIAN NONMEAT BALLS

These are real proof that it doesn't have to be meat to be Italian!

Mix well in a large bowl
> 1 LB. TOFU, MASHED WELL WITH A FORK
> 2 EGGS, LIGHTLY BEATEN
> ½ CUP FINE FRESH BREAD CRUMBS
> 2 TSP. BEEF FLAVORED BOUILLON
> ½ TSP. ONION SALT
> ½ TSP. ITALIAN SEASONING OR ¼ TSP. <u>EACH</u>
>    OREGANO AND BASIL
> ½ TSP. GARLIC POWDER
> 3 TBS. GRATED PARMESAN CHEESE
> 1 TBS. DEHYDRATED ONION FLAKES
> ¼ TSP. PEPPER
> ⅛ TSP. NUTMEG

Form into 1" balls.
Brown the balls in oil.
Use with your favorite spaghetti recipe or place the balls in an oiled baking dish and cover them half way with
> YOUR FAVORITE ITALIAN-STYLE TOMATO SAUCE

Bake at 350° for 30 minutes.
Makes about 30 balls.

# SPINACH PIE

Prepare your favorite unsweetened, double, 10" crust. (optional)
Steam until barely done
      10 – 12 OZ. SPINACH
Drain well.

Add

      1 LB. TOFU, MASHED WELL WITH A FORK
      2 EGGS, LIGHTLY BEATEN
      2½ CUPS GRATED CHEDDAR CHEESE
      1½ TSP. SALT

Turn into the prepared crust or a 10" oiled casserole.
If a crust is used, top with the upper crust, flute the edges and
prick with a fork.
Bake at 450° for 10 minutes, reduce heat to 350° and bake an
additional 45 – 50 minutes.
If a crust is not used, bake at 350° for 30 – 40 minutes.

# ITALIAN CHEESE PIE

**THE CRUST** (OPTIONAL)

Prepare your favorite unsweetened, single, 9" crust.
Bake at 425° for 10 minutes.

**THE FILLING**

Mix in a blender until smooth
>       2 EGGS
>       1 LB. TOFU
>       ¾ TSP. SALT
>       ¾ TSP. ITALIAN SEASONING
>         OR ¼ TSP. <u>EACH</u> OREGANO, BASIL AND THYME
>       ¼ TSP. GARLIC POWDER
>       1 CAN (8 OZ.) TOMATO SAUCE

Turn the tofu mixture into a large bowl.
Stir in
>       ½ CUP GRATED PARMESAN CHEESE
>       ½ CUP GRATED MOZZARELLA CHEESE

Spread evenly in the prepared crust or in a 9" casserole.
Top with
>       6 – 8 OZ. MOZZARELLA CHEESE, THINLY SLICED

Bake at 350° for 30 – 40 minutes or until set and browned.
Serves 4.

# BAKED ITALIAN EGGPLANT SKILLET

Sauté in a large oven-proof skillet over medium heat
  1 MEDIUM ONION, CHOPPED
  4 CLOVES GARLIC, MINCED

In

  2 TBS. OIL

Add

  1 EGGPLANT, DICED IN ¼" CUBES
  1 CAN (8 OZ.) TOMATO SAUCE
  ¼ CUP WATER
  2 TSP. CHICKEN FLAVORED BOUILLON
  ¾ TSP. ITALIAN SEASONING OR ¼ TSP. <u>EACH</u>
    OREGANO, BASIL AND THYME
  ¼ TSP. GARLIC POWDER

Bring to a boil, reduce heat, and simmer, covered for 10 minutes.
While the eggplant is simmering, mix together in a large bowl
  1 LB. TOFU, MASHED WELL WITH A FORK
  3 EGGS, LIGHTLY BEATEN
  1 CUP GRATED CHEESE

When the eggplant has simmered for 10 minutes, stir in the tofu mixture.
Sprinkle with
  GRATED PARMESAN CHEESE

Bake at 350° for 35 minutes.
Serves 4 – 5.

# TOFU NUT LOAF OR STUFFING

Sauté for about 5 minutes
> 1 ONION, CHOPPED
> 1½ CUPS CHOPPED CELERY
> 3 CLOVES GARLIC, MINCED

In
> 4 – 6 TBS. BUTTER*

Remove from heat.
Add
> 1 LB. TOFU, MASHED WELL WITH A FORK
> 2 CUPS COOKED MILLET** OR RICE
> 1 CUP CHOPPED WALNUTS
> 1 CUP CHOPPED CASHEWS
> ¼ CUP SESAME SEEDS, TOASTED
> 1 TSP. PARSLEY
> ¼ TSP. ROSEMARY
> ½ TSP. SAGE
> 1½ TSP. SALT
> ½ TSP. PEPPER
> 3 EGGS, LIGHTLY BEATEN

Turn into an oiled 9" x 5" loaf pan.
Bake at 350° for about 40 minutes.
Serves 6 – 8.

*If using as a stuffing, you may wish to add another 4 tbs. butter.
**See page 45.

# WEIGHT WATCHER'S MEXICAN STYLE LUNCH

Soak in a medium-sized, stainless steel or glass bowl for 30 minutes
  1 CUP CHOPPED ONION
  ½ CUP APPLE CIDER VINEGAR
Drain well.

Mix in a blender until smooth
  1 LB. TOFU
  2 CUPS TOMATO SAUCE
  1 TSP. SALT
  1 TSP. CUMIN
  ⅛ TSP. CLOVES
  2 CLOVES GARLIC

Turn the tofu mixture into a large bowl.
Stir in
  THE DRAINED ONION
  1 CUP FINELY CHOPPED BELL PEPPER
  1 CUP GRATED CHEDDAR CHEESE

Spread evenly in a 2 quart casserole.
Bake at 350° for 1 hour.
Makes 4 servings.

# CREAMED CORN CUSTARD

Mix in a blender until smooth
> 1 LB. TOFU
> 3 – 4 EGGS
> 2 TBS. BUTTER
> 2 TBS. HONEY
> ½ TSP. SALT
> ¼ – ½ TSP. PEPPER
> ¼ CUP WHOLEWHEAT FLOUR
> ½ CUP INSTANT NONFAT MILK POWDER

Add
> 2 CUPS WHOLE KERNEL CORN, COOKED AND
> DRAINED (SAVE THE LIQUOR)
> ¾ CUP CORN LIQUOR (OR WATER)

Blend again until the mixture resembles a fine grade of creamed corn.
Turn into an oiled 10" baking dish.
Bake at 350° for 50 – 60 minutes.
Serves 4.

# TOFU TAMALE PIE

Sauté in a 5 quart pan

    1 ONION, CHOPPED
    1 MEDIUM BELL PEPPER, CHOPPED
    3 LARGE CLOVES GARLIC, MINCED

In

    3 TBS. OIL

Remove from heat.
Stir in

    2 LBS. TOFU, MASHED WELL WITH A FORK
    2 CANS (16 OZ. EACH) TOMATOES, BROKEN UP
    1 CAN (4½ OZ.) CHOPPED BLACK OLIVES
    2 CUPS KERNEL CORN
    ¾ CUP WATER
    2 TBS. CHILI POWDER
    2 TBS. BEEF FLAVORED BOUILLON
    ¾ TSP. SALT
    ¾ TSP. GARLIC POWDER
    ½ TSP. CUMIN
    ¼ TSP. PEPPER
    1 CUP CORN MEAL

Bake at 350° for 45 minutes.
Remove from oven.
Top with

    8 OZ. MONTEREY JACK CHEESE, THINLY SLICED

Return to the oven for an additional 15 minutes.
Serves 6 – 8.

# TOFU CASSEROLE
# AL ITALIANO

Mix in a blender until smooth
>  1 LB. TOFU
>  3 EGGS
>  1 CAN (8 OZ.) TOMATO SAUCE
>  2 – 4 CLOVES GARLIC
>  2 TSP. BASIL
>  1 TSP. SALT
>  ¼ TSP. NUTMEG
>  2 TBS. ONION POWDER
>  ¼ TSP. PEPPER
>  2 – 4 TBS. GRATED PARMESAN CHEESE

Add and blend again
>  2 TBS. FLOUR

Add
>  1 BELL PEPPER, FINELY CHOPPED
>  1 CUP CHOPPED GREEN ONION

Mix in well with a long handled spoon.

Turn half the tofu mixture into an oiled 2 quart casserole.
Cover with half the slices from
>  8 OZ. MOZZARELLA CHEESE, THINLY SLICED

Spread the remaining tofu mixture over the cheese slices.
Top with the remaining cheese.
Bake at 350° for 50 – 60 minutes or until golden brown.
Serves 6.

# POTATO BAKE
# WITH CHEESE

Mix gently in a large bowl
      ½ CUP CHOPPED GREEN ONION
      2 CUPS COOKED POTATOES, SLICED OR DICED
      1 LB. TOFU, MASHED WELL WITH A FORK
      2 EGGS, LIGHTLY BEATEN
      1 CUP SOUR CREAM
      1 CUP GRATED CHEDDAR CHEESE
      2 TSP. SEASONED OR HERB SALT

Turn into an oiled 2 quart casserole.
Bake at 350° for 50 – 60 minutes.
Serves 4.

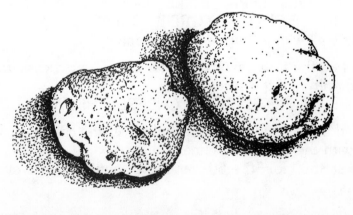

# TOFU QUICHE

*3/22/14*
*+ yum.*

## THE CRUST (OPTIONAL)

Mix together in a medium bowl → *I used seasoned crackers.*
> 35 ROMAN MEAL OR SALTINE LIKE CRACKERS,
> CRUSHED
> ¼ – ½ CUP MELTED BUTTER

Press into a 9" spring form pan.
Chill until needed.

## THE FILLING

Mix in a blender until smooth
> ½ CUP MILK
> 3 EGGS → *I used 4 eggs and 10 oz of tofu.*
> 1½ LBS. TOFU
> 3 TBS. FLOUR
> 2 TBS. ONION POWDER → *this is an ok amount.*
> 1 TSP. SALT
> 1 TSP. WORCESTERSHIRE SAUCE
> ¼ TSP. PEPPER OR CAYENNE

Add and mix in well with a long handled spoon
> 2 CUPS GRATED SWISS CHEESE – *I used 1 cup.*

Turn into the prepared crust or a 9" oiled casserole. *I added 1 cup chopped onion.*
Bake at 350° for 60 minutes.
Serves 6.

*I added sprinkle Parmesan.*

33

# ONION TORTE

### THE CRUST (OPTIONAL)

Mix together in a medium-sized bowl
>  35 ROMAN MEAL OR SALTINE LIKE CRACKERS, CRUSHED
>  ¼ – ½ CUP MELTED BUTTER

Press into an 8" or 9" spring form pan.
Chill until needed.

### THE FILLING

Sauté until golden
>  5 MEDIUM ONIONS, SLICED

In
>  2 – 3 TBS. BUTTER

Spread the onions evenly on the bottom of the crust or in the bottom of an oiled 9" baking dish.

Mix in a blender until smooth
>  4 EGGS
>  1 LB. TOFU
>  1¼ TSP. SALT
>  1 TSP. PARSLEY
>  ¼ TSP. PEPPER OR CAYENNE
>  ¼ TSP. BITTERS (optional)

Pour into a large bowl.

Continued

Stir in
     2 – 3 CUPS GRATED CHEDDAR CHEESE
Spread gently over the onions.

Dust with
     PAPRIKA

Bake at 350° for 50 – 60 minutes.
Serves 6.

# GREEN OLIVE CHILI CASSEROLE

Layer _half_ of each of the following ingredients, in order, in an oiled 9" x 13" baking dish

- 1 BAG (7 OZ.) NATURAL CORN CHIPS
- 2 CUPS GRATED MONTEREY JACK CHEESE
- 2 CUPS GRATED CHEDDAR CHEESE
- 2 CANS (4 OZ. EACH) CHOPPED GREEN CHILIS
- 1 CAN (15 OZ.) GREEN OLIVES (PITTED OR STUFFED), DRAINED AND SLICED

Repeat the layers.

Mix one of the following combinations in a blender until smooth

| | |
|---|---|
| 6 EGGS | 1 CAN (16 OZ.) |
| 2 CUPS MILK | TOMATO SAUCE |
| 1 LB. TOFU        OR | 1 LB. TOFU |
| 1 TSP. DRY | 6 EGGS |
| MUSTARD | 2 TSP. CUMIN |
| 1 TSP. SALT | 1½ TSP. ONION SALT |
| | ½ TSP. OREGANO |
| | ¼ TSP. PEPPER |

Pour your chosen mixture evenly over the layers.
Refrigerate for at least 4 hours. May be refrigerated overnight.
Bake at 350° for 1 hour.
Serves 8. Good hot or cold!

# SPICY SKILLET BAKE

Sauté in a large oven-proof skillet over medium heat
      1 LARGE ONION, FINELY CHOPPED
      1 LARGE BELL PEPPER, FINELY CHOPPED
In
      2 TBS. OIL
Remove from heat.

Stir in
      1 LB. TOFU, MASHED WELL WITH A FORK
      1 CAN (8 OZ.) TOMATO SAUCE
      4 EGGS, LIGHTLY BEATEN
      1½ TSP. CUMIN
      2 TSP. CHILI POWDER
      1 TSP. SALT
      ½ TSP. GARLIC POWDER
      1 CUP GRATED CHEESE

Bake at 375° for 45 minutes.
Serves 4 – 6.

# TOFU PAN PIZZA

Mix in a blender until smooth

    1 LB. TOFU
    2 EGGS
    1 TBS. OIL
    ½ TSP. SALT

Add and mix again

    1½ CUPS WHOLEWHEAT FLOUR
    2 TSP. BAKING POWDER

Spread the dough out on a 12" oiled pizza pan or baking sheet.
Spoon on **Special Sauce**.

Top with

    8 – 10 OZ. MOZZARELLA, GRATED OR THINLY
      SLICED.

Bake at 400° for 30 minutes.
Serves 4 – 6.

## SPECIAL SAUCE

Sauté

    1 CUP CHOPPED ONION
    1 CUP CHOPPED BELL PEPPER
    2 CLOVES GARLIC, MINCED

In

    3 TBS. OIL

Continued

Add

> 1 CAN (15 OZ.) TOMATO SAUCE
> ½ TSP. SALT
> 1 TSP. ITALIAN SEASONING OR ½ TSP. <u>EACH</u>
>   OREGANO AND BASIL

Bring to a boil, reduce heat, and simmer 20 – 30 minutes — until very thick.

# TOFU DIP

Mix in a blender until smooth
    8 OZ. TOFU
    1 CUP SOUR CREAM
    1 TBS. ONION SALT
    1 TBS. DEHYDRATED ONION FLAKES
    1½ TSP. GARLIC POWDER
    2 TBS. GRATED PARMESAN CHEESE

Add and mix in well with a long handled spoon
    1 TBS. DEHYDRATED ONION FLAKES

Refrigerate for several hours before serving.
Makes 2 cups.

# TOFU HUMMUS

This is an adaptation of an Armenian dish which is delicious either eaten on its own, served as a dip for raw veggies, or used as a spread for bread or crackers. If you are not already familiar with tahini (similar to peanut butter, but made from sesame seeds) this recipe will provide you with an opportunity to become so. It is available in some supermarkets, but most often found in delicatessens and health food stores. Sesame seeds are an ideal protein complement for tofu.

Mix in a blender until smooth. Use a spatula to keep the mixture in the blades if necessary.
>    1 LB. TOFU
>    1 CUP TAHINI
>    ¾ CUP LEMON JUICE
>    2 TSP. SALT
>    2 CLOVES GARLIC

Refrigerate for several hours before serving.
Serve garnished with
>    CHOPPED PARSLEY.

# FROZEN TOFU MAIN DISHES

# HUEVOS RANCHEROS

Sauté for about 5 minutes
>    1 ONION, CHOPPED
>    1 BELL PEPPER, CHOPPED
>    3 – 4 CLOVES GARLIC, MINCED

In
>    2 TBS. OIL (OLIVE, PREFERABLY)

Add
>    1 CAN (15 OZ.) TOMATO SAUCE
>    ½ CUP WATER
>    1 LB. FROZEN TOFU, THAWED, RINSED,
>      SQUEEZED DRY AND CRUMBLED
>    ½ TSP. OREGANO
>    ½ TSP. CHILI POWDER
>    ½ TSP. CUMIN
>    2 TSP. BEEF FLAVORED BOUILLON
>    ¼ TSP. PEPPER

Bring to a boil, reduce heat and simmer, covered, for 10 minutes.
Make four indentations in the thick tofu sauce; break an egg
into each one.
Simmer, covered, 5 – 10 minutes more — until the eggs are
poached as desired.
Spoon into 4 bowls.

# MEAL IN A SKILLET

Sauté for about 5 minutes
    1 MEDIUM ONION, CHOPPED
    ½ MEDIUM BELL PEPPER, CHOPPED
    2 – 4 CLOVES GARLIC, MINCED

In
    1 – 2 TBS. OLIVE OIL

Add
    1 CAN (28 OZ.) TOMATOES, BROKEN UP
    1 BAY LEAF
    ½ TSP. BASIL
    ½ TSP. OREGANO
    ½ TSP. SALT
    ¼ TSP. PEPPER
    ½ – 1 CUP SLICED MUSHROOMS
    1½ LBS. FROZEN TOFU, THAWED, RINSED,
      SQUEEZED DRY AND CRUMBLED

Bring to a boil, reduce heat, and simmer, covered, for 30 minutes.
Remove from heat and add slowly, stirring constantly
    2 – 4 EGGS, LIGHTLY BEATEN

Continue stirring until the entree is smooth and thickened.
Serves 4.
Good with millet.*

*Millet complements the protein in tofu extremely well. It is similar to rice in flavor, but millet has
more protein and iron and fewer calories. Millet is not readily available in all supermarkets, but it
can be found in natural food stores and health food stores as well as in Oriental specialty shops.
To prepare millet, use 3 – 3½ times as much water as grain. Cook, covered, for about 30 minutes.
For a nutty-flavored millet, sauté in a bit of oil before adding the water and cooking.

# BAKED CHILI RELLENO

Sauté

>    1 ONION, CHOPPED

In

>    1 TBS. OIL

Remove from heat and stir in

>    1½ LBS. FROZEN TOFU, THAWED, RINSED,
>      SQUEEZED DRY AND CRUMBLED
>    1 TSP. BEEF FLAVORED BOUILLON
>    ¼ TSP. SALT
>    ¼ TSP. PEPPER

Mix well in a medium-sized bowl

>    4 EGGS, LIGHTLY BEATEN
>    1½ CUPS MILK
>    ¼ CUP WHOLEWHEAT FLOUR
>    ¼ TSP. SALT
>    ¼ TSP. PEPPER

Layer _half_ of each of the following, in order, in an oiled 8" x 8" baking dish

>    2 CANS (4 OZ. EACH) CHOPPED GREEN CHILIS
>    2 CUPS GRATED CHEDDAR CHEESE
>    THE TOFU MIXTURE

Repeat the layers.
Pour the egg mixture evenly over the casserole.
Bake at 350° for 50 – 60 minutes or until a toothpick inserted in the center comes out clean.
Serves 4 – 6.

# CHILI CON TOFU

Sauté

  1 MEDIUM ONION, CHOPPED
  2 CLOVES GARLIC, MINCED

In

  2 – 3 TBS. OIL

Add

  2 CANS (16 OZ. EACH) TOMATOES, BROKEN UP
  3½ CUPS COOKED KIDNEY BEANS*
  1¼ CUPS BEAN LIQUOR (OR WATER)*
  2 TSP. BEEF FLAVORED BOUILLON
  2 TSP. CHILI POWDER (OR MORE, TO TASTE)
  ½ TSP. CUMIN
  ¾ TSP. SALT (OR ABOUT 1¼ TSP. IF THE BEANS
    USED HAVE NOT BEEN SALTED)
  1 BAY LEAF
  1 TSP. HONEY
  2 LBS. FROZEN TOFU, THAWED, RINSED,
    SQUEEZED DRY, AND CRUMBLED

Bring to a boil, reduce heat, and simmer, covered, for 1 hour.
Serves 8.

*2 cans (16 oz. each) kidney beans, undrained, can be substituted for cooked beans and bean liquor.

# ENCHILADAS

Best baked a day ahead and reheated.

## THE SAUCE

Sauté
> 1 LARGE ONION, CHOPPED
> 2 MEDIUM BELL PEPPERS, CHOPPED
> 4 CLOVES GARLIC, MINCED

In
> 1 – 3 TBS. OLIVE OIL

Add
> 3 CANS (8 OZ. EACH) TOMATO SAUCE
> 3 BAY LEAVES
> 2 TSP. BEEF FLAVORED BOUILLON
> 1 TSP. – 1 TBS. CUMIN POWDER (TO TASTE)
> ¼ TSP. CLOVES
> ¼ TSP. SALT

Bring to a boil, reduce heat and simmer, covered, for 30 minutes.

## THE FILLING

Soak in a large stainless steel or glass bowl for 30 minutes.
> 2 SMALL ONIONS, CHOPPED
> ½ CUP APPLE CIDER OR WINE VINEGAR

Drain well.

Continued

Stir in

>2 LBS. FROZEN TOFU, THAWED, RINSED,
>SQUEEZED DRY AND CRUMBLED
>2 CANS (4½ OZ. EACH) CHOPPED BLACK OLIVES
>1 TSP. SALT
>1 TSP. GARLIC POWDER
>2 CUPS GRATED SHARP CHEDDAR CHEESE

## THE GARNISHES

>1½ CUPS SHREDDED ICEBERG LETTUCE
>2 CUPS GRATED SHARP CHEDDAR CHEESE
>8 HARD BOILED EGGS, SLICED IN ROUNDS

## ASSEMBLING THE ENCHILADAS

>12 NATURAL FLOUR TORTILLAS

Heat a tortilla in an ungreased skillet over medium-hot heat until soft (a few seconds on each side).
Dip the heated tortilla into the prepared sauce.

Continued

Fill each tortilla with
  ½ CUP FILLING

Garnish with
  2 TBS. SHREDDED LETTUCE
  1 – 2 TBS. GRATED CHEESE
  6 – 7 EGG ROUNDS

Roll the tortilla around the filling.
When all the tortillas have been filled, place them close together, seam-side down, in a large baking dish.
Cover with the remaining prepared sauce.

Top with the remaining garnish cheese plus
  2 CUPS GRATED MONTEREY JACK CHEESE

Bake, covered, at 350° for 1 hour.
Refrigerate overnight.
Reheat, covered, at 350° for 30 – 35 minutes.
Serves 10 – 12.

# STUFFED BELL PEPPERS

Sauté for about 5 minutes
> 1 LARGE ONION, CHOPPED
> 2 CLOVES GARLIC, MINCED

In
> 1 – 2 TBS. OLIVE OIL

Remove from heat and stir in
> 1 LB. FROZEN TOFU, THAWED, RINSED,
>   SQUEEZED DRY AND CRUMBLED
> 1 CAN (15 OZ.) TOMATO SAUCE
> ½ TSP. SALT
> ¼ TSP. BASIL
> ¼ TSP. SAGE
> ¼ TSP. PEPPER
> ½ CUP GRATED SHARP CHEESE

When slightly cooled add slowly, stirring constantly
> 3 EGGS, LIGHTLY BEATEN

Spoon the mixture into
> 4 LARGE BELL PEPPERS, STEMMED AND SEEDED

Place the peppers upright in a baking dish and pour in ¾ cup boiling water.
Bake at 350° for 1 hour or until the peppers are tender when pierced with a fork.
(Add more water during baking if necessary.)

# TOFU A LA KING

Sauté in a large skillet over medium heat
> 1 MEDIUM ONION, CHOPPED
> ¼ CUP CHOPPED GREEN PEPPER
> 3 CUPS THINLY SLICED MUSHROOMS

In
> 2 TBS. BUTTER OR OIL

Mix in a blender until smooth
> 3 CUPS MILK
> 8 OZ. CREAM CHEESE, SOFTENED
> 2 – 3 TBS. DRY SHERRY
> 1 CUP INSTANT NONFAT MILK POWDER
> 3 TBS. ARROWROOT OR CORNSTARCH
> 1 TBS. + 1 TSP. CHICKEN FLAVORED BOUILLON
> ¼ TSP. SALT
> ¼ TSP. PEPPER

Pour the blended ingredients into the skillet.
Add
> 2 LBS. FROZEN TOFU, THAWED, RINSED,
>   SQUEEZED DRY AND CRUMBLED

Mix well.
Bring to a boil and simmer, stirring constantly, until thickened (about 2 minutes).
Serves 4. Good over hot millet.*

*See page 45.

# POTATO CHEESE CHOWDER

Sauté for 3 minutes
    1 MEDIUM ONION, CHOPPED
    2 – 4 CLOVES GARLIC, MINCED

In
    1 – 3 TBS. OIL

Add and sauté for an additional 2 minutes
    3 MEDIUM POTATOES, DICED IN ½" CUBES

Add
    2 CANS (8 OZ. EACH) TOMATO SAUCE
    4 CUPS WATER
    1 LB. FROZEN TOFU, THAWED, RINSED,
      SQUEEZED DRY AND CRUMBLED
    ¼ TSP. SALT
    1 TSP. BEEF FLAVORED BOUILLON

Bring to a boil, reduce heat and simmer, covered, for 20 minutes or until the potatoes are cooked but not mushy.

Remove from heat and stir in
    1¼ CUPS GRATED CHEDDAR CHEESE

Stir until the cheese is melted and well integrated with the other ingredients.
Serves 4 – 6.

*A winner!*

# NOODLELESS LASAGNA

## THE SAUCE

Sauté

    4 ONIONS, CHOPPED
    4 CLOVES GARLIC, MINCED

*can leave these out & it's still delicious*

In

    ¼ CUP OLIVE OIL

Add

    2 CANS (15 OZ. EACH) TOMATO SAUCE
    1 CAN (16 OZ.) TOMATOES, BROKEN UP
    2 TSP. BEEF FLAVORED BOUILLON
    2 TSP. OREGANO
    1½ TSP. SALT *omit*

Bring to a boil, reduce heat, and simmer, covered, for 30 minutes.

## THE FILLING

While the sauce is simmering, mix together in a large bowl
    1 LB. TOFU, MASHED WELL WITH A FORK
    1 EGG
    ½ CUP GRATED PARMESAN CHEESE
    2 CUPS GRATED MOZZARELLA CHEESE

*1 can shrooms & ¼ c. sunflower seeds*

*1 ¾ c. ½ c. cottage cheese*

*4 pinches or 1 tsp.* *Rosemary — crushed.*

Continued

54

## THE "NOODLES"

Slice in strips about as thick as lasagna noodles
> 1 LB. FROZEN TOFU, THAWED, RINSED, AND
> SQUEEZED DRY

*and 2 zucchini*

## ASSEMBLING THE LASAGNA

Spread about ⅓ of the simmered tomato sauce in the bottom of an
oiled 9" x 13" baking dish.    *or 8" square dish*
Place half the tofu slices on the sauce.
Cover with half the filling.
Repeat the layers.
Pour the remaining sauce evenly over the casserole.

Dust with
> GRATED PARMESAN CHEESE

Bake, covered, at 350° for 45 minutes. *to 60 minutes*
Let stand for 10 minutes before cutting.
Serves 8 – 10.

# STUFFED CABBAGE LEAVES

### THE LEAVES

> 1 MEDIUM CABBAGE

Remove the core from the cabbage and steam for 5 minutes over boiling water.
Carefully peel off 8 – 12 outer leaves.

### THE FILLING

Sauté

> 1 MEDIUM ONION, CHOPPED
> 1 BELL PEPPER, CHOPPED
> 4 LARGE CLOVES GARLIC, MINCED

In

> 3 TBS. OLIVE OIL

Remove from heat and stir in

> 1 – 1½ LBS. FROZEN TOFU, THAWED, RINSED,
>    SQUEEZED DRY AND CRUMBLED
> 1 CAN (15 OZ.) TOMATO SAUCE
> 3 EGGS, LIGHTLY BEATEN
> 1 CUP COOKED RICE
> ¼ CUP RAISINS
> ½ TSP. SALT
> ½ TSP. PAPRIKA
> ¼ TSP. PEPPER

Continued

## THE GARNISH

Mix well in a large bowl
>  1 MEDIUM ONION, SLICED IN RINGS OR HALF RINGS
>  1 MEDIUM BELL PEPPER, CHOPPED
>  4 LARGE CLOVES GARLIC, MINCED
>  ¼ CUP RAISINS

## THE SAUCE

Mix together in a medium bowl
>  1 CAN (15 OZ.) TOMATO SAUCE
>  ¼ CUP WATER
>  ¼ TSP. SALT
>  ¼ TSP. PEPPER

## ASSEMBLING THE CABBAGE LEAVES

Put ½ cup of the filling in the center of either 1 large or 2 smaller overlapping leaves.

Fold the ends of the leaf in and roll it around the filling.

Place the rolled leaves close together in an oiled, 5 quart covered casserole.

Spread the garnish evenly over the rolls.

Pour the sauce (mixed with any remaining filling) over the casserole.

Bake, covered, at 350° for 1 hour.

Serve with a large spoon to avoid breaking the rolls.

# CREPES WITH TOFU AND MUSHROOMS

The perpetually pleasing crepe houses tofu in simplicity and elegance — a lovely gift for company.

## THE CREPES

Mix in a blender until smooth
> 3 LARGE EGGS
> ½ CUP MILK
> 2 TBS. MELTED BUTTER
> ¼ TSP. HONEY
> ½ CUP FLOUR
> DASH OF SALT
> PEPPER TO TASTE

Set aside for 1 hour.
Heat a 7" crepe pan.
Coat the pan lightly with butter.
Cover the bottom of the pan with 3 TBS. of the crepe batter.
Swirl and tilt the pan to distribute the batter evenly.
When the bottom of the crepe is lightly browned, turn and brown the other side.
Stack the finished crepes on a plate.
Makes 8 crepes.

Continued

## THE FILLING

Sauté
>     2 CUPS SLICED MUSHROOMS
>     ½ CUP CHOPPED GREEN ONION
>     1 CLOVE GARLIC MINCED

In
>     2 TBS. BUTTER OR OIL

Remove from the pan. Set aside.

In the same pan, over low heat, mix together
>     2 TBS. BUTTER OR OIL
>     2 TBS. FLOUR
>     2 TSP. CHICKEN FLAVORED BOUILLON

Add slowly, stirring constantly
>     ½ CUP MILK

Cook, stirring constantly, until thickened.

Remove from heat and stir in
>     1 LB. FROZEN TOFU, THAWED, RINSED,
>         SQUEEZED DRY AND CRUMBLED
>     ½ OF THE MUSHROOM MIXTURE
>         (BUT ALL ITS LIQUID)
>     ½ CUP SOUR CREAM
>     2 TBS. DRY SHERRY
>     ½ TSP. SALT
>     ¼ TSP. PEPPER OR A FEW GRAINS CAYENNE

Continued

## ASSEMBLING THE CREPES

Spoon ⅛ of the filling down the center of each crepe.
Fold the ends in and roll the crepe around the filling.
Place 2 crepes, seam side down, on each of 4 broiler-proof plates.

Top with
      ½ CUP GRATED CHEESE
      THE REMAINING MUSHROOMS

Broil 4 inches from heat until the cheese melts.
Serve immediately.
Serves 4.

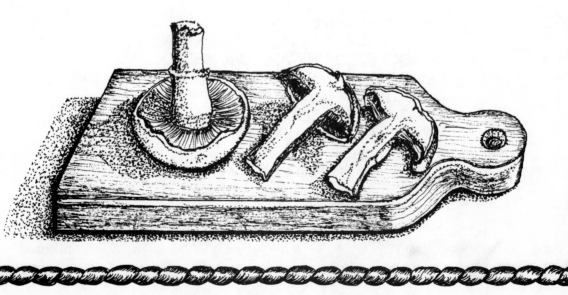

# CHEESY ZUCCHINI PUFF

Steam until tender
    3 MEDIUM ZUCCHINI, CUT IN SLICES OR CHUNKS

Mix together in a large bowl
    1 CUP (4 OZ.) GRATED CHEDDAR CHEESE
    12 OZ. FROZEN TOFU, THAWED, RINSED,
      SQUEEZED DRY AND CRUMBLED
    2 EGGS, LIGHTLY BEATEN
    ¾ TSP. SALT
    ¾ TSP. DILL WEED
    ½ CUP CROUTONS — *I used leftover rice*

Add and stir gently
    THE ZUCCHINI, WELL DRAINED

*— try adding nuts sometime*

Turn into a shallow, oiled 1½ quart casserole.
Bake at 350° for 30 minutes.
Serves 3 as a main dish, 6 as a side dish.

# EGGPLANT AND FROZEN TOFU IN CASSEROLE

Sauté
  1 ONION, CHOPPED
  1 SMALL BELL PEPPER, CHOPPED

In
  1 – 2 TBS. OLIVE OIL

Remove from heat and stir in
  1 CAN (16 OZ.) TOMATOES, BROKEN UP
  1 LB. FROZEN TOFU, THAWED, RINSED, SQUEEZED
    DRY AND CRUMBLED
  ½ TSP. SALT
  ¼ TSP. PEPPER

Spread in the bottom of a 9" x 13" baking dish
  ¼ OF A CAN (15 OZ.) TOMATO SAUCE

Top with <u>half</u> the slices from
  1 MEDIUM EGGPLANT, CUT IN ¼" ROUNDS

Spread <u>half</u> the tofu mixture on the eggplant rounds.
Cover the tofu mixture with <u>half</u> the slices from
  8 – 10 OZ. MOZZARELLA CHEESE, THINLY SLICED

Repeat eggplant, tofu and cheese layers.

Continued

Mix in a medium bowl

      THE REST OF THE TOMATO SAUCE
      ½ TSP. OREGANO
      ½ TSP. BASIL
      ¼ CUP WATER

Pour evenly over the casserole.
Top with

      2 TBS. GRATED PARMESAN CHEESE

Bake, covered, at 375° for 20 minutes.
Remove cover and bake for an additional 20 minutes.
Let stand for 15 minutes before cutting.
Serves 4 – 6.

# TOFU BREADS

65

# TOFU PANCAKES

Mix in a blender until smooth
      1½ CUPS MILK
      3 EGGS
      1 LB. TOFU
      1 TSP. – 1 TBS. OIL
      2 TBS. HONEY
      1 TSP. BAKING POWDER
      1 TSP. VANILLA
      ¼ TSP. SALT

Add and blend again
      1 CUP WHOLEWHEAT FLOUR

Bake on a lightly oiled, medium-hot griddle until done.
Makes about 18 pancakes.

# VERY SPECIAL FRENCH TOAST

Mix in a blender until smooth
>  6 – 8 EGGS
>  1½ LBS. TOFU
>  ½ TSP. CINNAMON
>  ½ TSP. SALT
>  ¼ CUP HONEY
>  2 TSP. VANILLA

Place in a single layer in the bottom of an oiled 9" x 13" pan
>  6  SLICES OF BREAD

Pour the tofu mixture evenly over the bread.
Sprinkle with
>  ½ TSP. CINNAMON

Bake at 350° for 30 minutes or until set .
Serve with maple syrup if desired.
Serves 6.

## APPLESAUCE VARIATION

Before pouring the tofu mixture over the bread, spoon ⅓ cup thick applesauce on each slice.

# PAN-FRIED CORN CAKES

Mix together in a large bowl
> 1 CUP TOFU, MASHED WELL WITH A FORK
> 1 EGG, LIGHTLY BEATEN
> 1/3 CUP MELTED BUTTER
> 1/4 CUP MILK
> 3/4 CUP WHOLEWHEAT FLOUR
> 3/4 TSP. SALT
> 2 CUPS WHOLE KERNEL CORN
> 2 TBS. CHOPPED GREEN ONION
> 1 1/2 TSP. BAKING POWDER
> 3/4 TSP. SALT
> 1/4 TSP. PEPPER

Drop by tablespoons onto a hot, oiled griddle.
Fry to a golden brown on both sides.
Makes 14 – 16 cakes.

# TOFU CHAPATIS

Mix in a blender until smooth
>      1 LB. TOFU
>      ½ CUP BUTTER
>      1½ TSP. SALT
>      2 TBS. BAKING POWDER

Turn into a large bowl.
Stir in
>      3 CUPS WHOLEWHEAT FLOUR

Beat the dough for about 1 minute, until it becomes somewhat smooth and elastic.
Divide the dough into 16 equal parts.
Roll each part into an 8" round on a floured surface.
Bake each chapati in an ungreased skillet over medium-high heat until done but not browned.
Stack the finished chapatis on a plate.
Makes 16 chapatis.

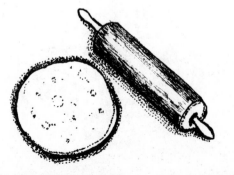

# TOFU WAFFLES

Mix in a blender until smooth
      4 EGGS
      ¾ CUP MILK OR WATER
      1 LB. TOFU
      2 TBS. HONEY
      ¼ TSP. SALT
      1 TSP. BAKING POWDER
      1 TSP. VANILLA

Add and blend again
      ¾ CUP WHOLEWHEAT FLOUR

Bake in a preheated waffle iron according to manufacturer's directions.
Stir the batter before pouring each waffle.
Makes 4 waffles.

70

# EGGLESS WAFFLES

Mix in a blender until smooth
  1¼ CUPS MILK
  1 LB. TOFU
  2 TBS. HONEY
  ¼ TSP. SALT
  1 TSP. BAKING POWDER
  1 TSP. VANILLA

Add and blend again
  1 CUP WHOLEWHEAT FLOUR

Bake in a preheated waffle iron according to manufacturer's directions.
Stir the batter before pouring each waffle.
Makes 4 large waffles.

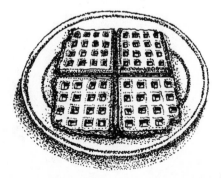

# WEIGHT WATCHER'S WAFFLE

Mix in a blender until smooth
    1 LB. TOFU
    4 EGGS
    2 TBS. HONEY
    1 TSP. VANILLA
    DASH SALT
    ¼ CUP WHOLEWHEAT FLOUR

Bake in a preheated waffle iron according to manufacturer's directions.
Stir the batter before pouring each waffle.
Makes 4 waffles.

# CAROB DESSERT WAFFLES

Mix in a blender until smooth
    ½ CUP MILK
    ½ CUP LIGHT MOLASSES
    ¼ CUP HONEY
    3 EGGS
    1 LB. TOFU
    4 TBS. CAROB POWDER
    3 TBS. OIL
    ¼ TSP. SALT
    1½ TSP. BAKING POWDER

Add and blend again
    1 CUP WHOLEWHEAT FLOUR

Bake in a preheated waffle iron according to manufacturer's directions.
Stir the batter before pouring each waffle.
Makes 4 waffles.

# TOFU RAISIN BREAD

Mix well in a large bowl.
>2 CUPS WHOLEWHEAT FLOUR
>½ CUP RAISINS

Mix in a blender until smooth
>2 EGGS
>1 LB. TOFU
>¼ CUP HONEY
>¼ CUP BUTTER
>4 TSP. BAKING POWDER
>¼ TSP. BAKING SODA
>¼ TSP. SALT

Pour the blended ingredients into the flour mixture. Stir well.
Turn into a buttered and floured 8" spring form pan.
Bake at 350° for 45 minutes or until a toothpick inserted into the center comes out clean.
Cool 10 minutes in the pan; remove to a rack.
Great with apricot preserves!

# TOFU BROWN BREAD

Mix well in a large bowl
>1 CUP CORN MEAL
>1 CUP RYE FLOUR
>1 CUP WHOLEWHEAT FLOUR
>1 CUP RAISINS

Mix in a blender until smooth
>2 EGGS
>1 LB. TOFU
>¾ CUP LIGHT MOLASSES
>1 TSP. SALT
>2 TSP. BAKING SODA
>1 TSP. LEMON JUICE

Pour the blended ingredients into the flour mixture.
Beat well with a spoon (or use an electric mixer.)
Turn into 2 buttered 1 quart cans. Fill ¾ full.
Cover the cans with aluminum foil and tie, tape or rubberband securely in place.
Place the cans on a rack (or a vegetable steamer) in a deep pot.
Add enough water to come up 2" on the sides of the cans. Cover the pot.
Steam for 3 hours. (The water should continue to boil gently throughout the steaming process. Add more water if it gets low.)
Cool for 10 minutes. Remove from the cans.
Serve hot.

# DUMPLINGS

Mix in a blender until smooth
> 8 OZ. TOFU
> 1 EGG
> 2 TSP. BAKING POWDER
> ¼ TSP. SALT

Add
> 2 SPRIGS FRESH PARSLEY, FINELY CHOPPED
> ½ CUP WHOLEWHEAT FLOUR

Blend again. Use a spatula to keep the mixture in the blades if necessary.

Drop by teaspoonfuls onto the top of a stew or a thick soup.

Cover tightly and simmer the stew or soup for 15 – 20 minutes while the dumplings steam.

Don't peak during the first 15 minutes!

# YORKSHIRE PUDDING

Preheat the oven to 400°.
Mix in a blender until smooth
      3 EGGS
      1 LB. TOFU
      1 TSP. SALT

Add and mix again
      ¾ CUP UNBLEACHED WHITE FLOUR

Melt in a 9" x 13" baking dish in the preheating oven
      ½ CUP (1 CUBE) BUTTER

Pour the tofu mixture slowly into the baking dish. DO NOT STIR.
Bake for 20 minutes.
Reduce heat to 350° and bake for an additional 10 – 15 minutes.
Cut into squares and serve immediately.
Makes 4 generous servings.

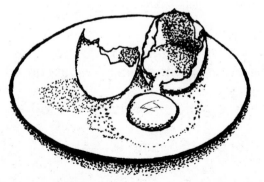

# TOFU PARMESAN CRESCENTS

Mix in a blender until smooth
  1 LB. TOFU
  ¾ CUP BUTTER, SOFTENED
  ¼ CUP PARMESAN CHEESE
  1 TSP. SALT
  2 TSP. BAKING POWDER

Pour into a large bowl.
Using an electric mixer, beat in
  2 CUPS WHOLEWHEAT FLOUR

Beat the dough for about 1 minute, until it becomes elastic and smooth.
Divide the dough into 4 equal parts.
Roll each part into a 10" round.
Sprinkle with
  GRATED PARMESAN CHEESE

Cut into 8 wedges.
Starting at the wider edge, roll up each wedge.
Place with the center point down, 2" apart on an oiled baking sheet.
Tuck the ends in slightly and curve down to form a crescent shape.
Bake at 375° for 30 – 35 minutes.
Makes 32 rolls.

# SESAME BREAD STICKS

Mix in a blender until smooth
>   1 LB. TOFU
>   ¾ CUP BUTTER, SOFTENED
>   1½ TSP. SALT
>   2½ TSP. BAKING POWDER

Pour into a large bowl.
Using an electric mixer, beat in
>   ½ CUP TOASTED SESAME SEEDS
>   2¼ – 2½ CUPS WHOLEWHEAT FLOUR

Beat the dough for 1 – 1½ minutes, until it becomes elastic and smooth.
Divide the dough in 32 parts.
Roll each part into a stick about 4" – 5" long.
Place 1" apart on an oiled baking sheet.
Bake at 375° for 30 – 35 minutes.
Serve warm or cool.
Makes 32 sticks.

# CORNBREAD OR MUFFINS

Preheat the oven to 425°.

Mix in a blender until smooth
> 1 LB. TOFU
> 2 EGGS
> 3 TBS. OIL
> ¼ CUP HONEY
> 1 CUP INSTANT NONFAT MILK POWDER
> ¼ CUP WHOLEWHEAT FLOUR
> 1 TSP. SALT
> 1½ TSP. BAKING POWDER
> ½ TSP. BAKING SODA

Pour into a large bowl.

Stir in
> 1½ CUPS CORN MEAL

Turn into an oiled 9" x 9" pan or into 12 oiled muffin tins.
Bake at 425° for 25 – 30 minutes. (Muffins will take less time.)
Great served piping hot with molasses!

# CINNAMON OAT MUFFINS

Mix well in a large bowl
> 1 CUP WHOLEWHEAT FLOUR
> 1 CUP ROLLED OATS
> ¼ CUP RAISINS (optional)

Mix in a blender until smooth
> 8 OZ. TOFU
> 2 EGGS
> ¼ CUP OIL
> ½ CUP HONEY
> 1 – 1½ TSP. CINNAMON
> ½ TSP. SALT
> 2 TSP. BAKING POWDER
> ¼ TSP. BAKING SODA

Pour the blended ingredients into the flour mixture. Stir well.
Fill oiled muffin tins ⅔ full.
Bake at 425° for 12 – 15 minutes.
Makes 12 muffins.

# CRISPY CRUMBLES
# OR TOFU CROUTONS

Cut into ½" squares
>    1 LB. FROZEN TOFU, THAWED, RINSED,
>    AND SQUEEZED DRY

Season as desired.
Toast in a broiler or a toaster oven on a lightly oiled baking sheet until dried and crunchy. Turn as needed.

## BUTTERY CROUTON VARIATION

After the tofu has toasted toss it with
>    2 – 3 TBS. MELTED BUTTER

Return it to the oven and bake at 350° for an additional 10 – 15 minutes.

## CHEESY CROUTON VARIATION

Sprinkle hot toasted tofu squares with
>    1½ TBS. FINELY GRATED CHEESE

# "BREADLESS" TOAST

Slice into bread shaped pieces about ½" wide
    1 LB. FROZEN TOFU, THAWED, RINSED,
    AND SQUEEZED DRY

Toast on each side in a broiler or a toaster oven on a lightly oiled baking sheet until browned and crunchy.
Once toasted, tofu toast can be reheated in a conventional pop-up toaster.

# TOFU DESSERTS

# BEST-EVER RICE PUDDING

Mix in a blender until smooth
    1 LB. TOFU
    3 EGGS
    1 CUP HONEY
    2 TSP. LEMON JUICE
    ½ TSP. GRATED LEMON RIND
    1 TBS. VANILLA
    ½ TSP. SALT
    ½ TSP. CINNAMON

Pour into a large bowl.
Stir in
    1 CUP COOKED RICE
    1 CUP UNSWEETENED COCONUT
    ¾ CUP RAISINS

Turn into an oiled 2 quart casserole.
Bake at 350° for 1 hour.
Serves 6 – 8. Good hot or cold.

# LEMONY BREAD PUDDING

Mix in a blender until smooth
     4 EGGS
     1 LB. TOFU
     1 CUP HONEY
     ½ CUP WATER OR MILK
     2 TBS. LEMON JUICE
     1 TSP. GRATED LEMON RIND
     ¼ TSP. SALT

Add and mix gently with a long-handled spoon
     2 CUPS DRIED BREAD CUBES (½")

Pour into a buttered 2 quart casserole.
Sprinkle with
     NUTMEG (optional)

Bake at 350° for 35 – 45 minutes.
Serves 4.

# TOFU MINI-PIES

Mix in a blender until smooth. Use a spatula to keep the dough in the blades if necessary.
> 1 CUP BUTTER
> 1 LB. VERY FRESH TOFU
> ¼ TSP. SALT

Turn into a large bowl and stir in
> 2 – 2½ CUPS WHOLEWHEAT FLOUR

Work the mixture until a soft dough is formed.
Cover and chill thoroughly.
Using a floured rolling pin, roll the dough out into a rectangle approximately 18" x 24".
Cut into 3" squares.

In the center of each square drop
> 1 TSP. PRESERVES

Fold the dough over to form a triangle and press the edges together to seal.
Prick and bake on an oiled sheet at 375° for 30 minutes.

# TOFU CHEESECAKE

Prepare your favorite cheesecake crumb crust in an 8" spring form pan. (optional)

Mix in a blender until smooth
      2 EGGS
      1 LB. VERY FRESH TOFU
      1 CUP HONEY
      8 OZ. CREAM CHEESE, SOFTENED
      3 TBS. LEMON JUICE
      1½ TSP. VANILLA
      DASH OF SALT

Turn into the prepared crust or a lightly buttered 8" baking dish.
Bake at 350° for 1 hour.
Chill thoroughly.

# TOFU CUSTARD

Mix in a blender until smooth
>  4 EGGS
>  1 LB. VERY FRESH TOFU
>  1 CUP HONEY
>  ½ CUP MILK
>  ¼ TSP. SALT
>  1 TBS. VANILLA
>  1 TSP. LEMON JUICE

Pour into either custard cups or a 2 quart casserole.

Sprinkle with
>  NUTMEG

Place the cups or the casserole in a large pan.
Pour water into the pan until it is half way up the sides of the custard dish(es).
Bake custard cups at 350° for 25 – 35 minutes or until set.
Bake the 2 quart casserole at 350° for 45 minutes to 1 hour.
Serve thoroughly chilled.
Makes 8 servings.

### LEMON CUSTARD

Prepare **Tofu Custard**. Reduce the vanilla to 1 tsp. Omit the nutmeg sprinkle.
Add

      2 TSP. GRATED LEMON RIND
      2 TBS. LEMON JUICE

### ALMOND CUSTARD

Prepare **Tofu Custard**. Reduce the vanilla to 1 tsp. Omit the lemon juice and the nutmeg sprinkle.
Add

      ½ TSP. ALMOND EXTRACT

### COCONUT CUSTARD

Prepare **Tofu Custard**. Omit the nutmeg sprinkle.
Add

      ½ CUP SHREDDED UNSWEETENED COCONUT

### CUSTARD PIE

Prepare your favorite single 9" crust.
Partially bake the crust at 425° for 8 minutes.
Reduce the oven temperature to 350°.
Pour any of the above custards into the partially baked crust.
Continue baking at 350° for 45 minutes, or until set.

# PUMPKIN PUDDING

Mix in a blender until smooth
> 2 CUPS COOKED PUMPKIN
> 1 LB. VERY FRESH TOFU
> 1 CUP HONEY
> ⅓ CUP ORANGE JUICE
> 1 CUP INSTANT NONFAT MILK POWDER
> 4 EGGS
> ¼ TSP. SALT
> 1 TBS. CINNAMON
> 1 TSP. GRATED ORANGE RIND
> ½ TSP. GINGER
> ¼ TSP. CLOVES
> 2 TSP. VANILLA

Pour the blended ingredients into a 9" square baking dish.
Bake at 350° for 1 hour or until a knife inserted in the center comes out clean.
Chill thoroughly.

# STEAMED
# CHRISTMAS PUDDING

Mix well in a large bowl
>1½ CUPS WHOLEWHEAT FLOUR
>3½ TSP. BAKING POWDER

Add and mix again
>1 CUP CHOPPED DATES OR FIGS
>1 CUP CHOPPED WALNUTS

Mix in a blender until smooth
>1 EGG
>1 LB. TOFU
>½ CUP HONEY
>½ CUP LIGHT MOLASSES
>2 TBS. OIL
>½ TSP. VANILLA
>¼ TSP. SALT

Pour the blended ingredients into the flour mixture. Mix well.
Turn into a buttered 5 pound honey can. Fill ¾ full.
Cover the can with aluminum foil and tie, tape, or rubber band securely in place.
Place the can on a rack (or a vegetable steamer) in a deep pot. Add enough boiling water to come half way up the sides of the can. Cover the pot.
Steam for 2 hours. (The water should continue to boil gently throughout the steaming process. Add more water if it gets low.)
Cool for 10 minutes. Remove from the can. Serve hot or cold.

# SERAPHINA'S CARROT CAKE

Mix in a blender until smooth
>1 EGG
>½ CUP OIL
>1 CUP HONEY
>8 OZ. TOFU
>2 TSP. CINNAMON
>2 TSP. BAKING SODA
>2 TSP. VANILLA
>½ TSP. SALT

Pour into a large bowl.
Using an electric mixer, beat in
>¾ CUP GRATED CARROT
>2 CUPS WHOLEWHEAT FLOUR

Stir in
>1 CUP CHOPPED NUTS

Turn into two 8" oiled and floured cake pans or fill 18 well oiled muffin tins ⅔ full.
Bake at 325° for 40 – 45 minutes for cake rounds, 30 – 35 for cupcakes.
When cool, frost with **Seraphina's Cream Cheese Frosting**, if desired.

## CAROB CARROT CAKE

Prepare **Seraphina's Carrot Cake**.
Omit the cinnamon.
Add
    6 TBS. CAROB POWDER

Bake as directed above.

## SERAPHINA'S CREAM CHEESE FROSTING

Beat with an electric mixer until creamy and easy to spread
    1 CUP CREAM CHEESE
    2 TBS. HONEY
    2 TSP. VANILLA

# SPICY TOFU COOKIES

Mix well in a large bowl
  1½ CUPS WHOLEWHEAT FLOUR
  ½ CUP RAISINS
  ½ CUP FINELY CHOPPED WALNUTS
  ½ CUP CHOPPED DATES
  ½ TSP. BAKING SODA

Mix in a blender until smooth
  ½ CUP BUTTER, SOFTENED
  ⅔ CUP HONEY
  1 EGG
  8 OZ. TOFU
  1 TSP. GINGER
  1 TSP. CINNAMON
  ½ TSP. NUTMEG
  ½ TSP. SALT
  1 TSP. VANILLA

Pour the blended ingredients into the flour mixture. Stir well.
Drop by teaspoonfuls onto an oiled baking sheet.
Bake at 400° for 10 – 15 minutes.

# SIMPLY SUPER FRUIT COBBLER

Prepare your favorite fruit filling in an 8" baking dish.
Bake at 350° until bubbly.
Remove from oven.
Spoon **Cobbler Topping** in a fairly even layer on top of the fruit.
Bake at 350° for 30 minutes.
Serve warm with cream or vanilla ice cream.

## COBBLER TOPPING

Mix together well in a medium-sized bowl
>     4 OZ. TOFU
>     1 TBS. BUTTER, SOFTENED

Add and mix again
>     1 EGG
>     1 TBS. HONEY
>     1 TSP. BAKING POWDER
>     ¼ TSP. SALT

Stir in
>     ¾ CUP WHOLEWHEAT FLOUR

Mix until well blended.

# ZABAGLIONE

A light, chilled wine custard. A very adult dessert.

Mix in a blender until smooth
> 3 EGG YOLKS
> 12 OZ. VERY FRESH TOFU
> ⅓ CUP HONEY
> ½ CUP MARSALA OR DRY SHERRY WINE
> 1½ TSP. VANILLA
> ⅛ TSP. SALT
> ⅛ TSP. NUTMEG

Whip in a large bowl until stiff
> 3 EGG WHITES

Gently fold the blended ingredients into the egg whites.
Pour into either an 8" x 8" casserole or custard cups.

Sprinkle with
> CINNAMON

Place the cups or the casserole in a large pan. Pour water into the pan until it is half way up the sides of the custard dish(es).
Bake at 350° for 30 – 35 minutes or until a knife inserted in the center comes out clean.
Serve thoroughly chilled.

Garnish with
> SLIVERED TOASTED ALMONDS

Serves 6.

# MELLOW PUDDING

Mix in a blender until smooth
      2 EGGS
      1 LB. VERY FRESH TOFU
      ½ CUP BUTTER
      1 CUP LIGHT MOLASSES
      1 CUP HONEY
      ½ TSP. BAKING SODA

Add and blend again
      ½ CUP WHOLEWHEAT FLOUR

Turn into an oiled 2 quart casserole.
Bake at 350° for 45 minutes or until firm.
Serve with whipped cream.

## FRUIT VARIATION

Before baking, stir in
      1 CUP FINELY CHOPPED WALNUTS
      1 CUP RAISINS OR CHOPPED PITTED DATES

Bake and serve as directed.

# CAROB PUDDING OR PIE FILLING

Soften
>2 TBS. UNFLAVORED GELATIN

In
>½ CUP WATER

Heat to dissolve thoroughly.

Mix in a blender until smooth
>1 LB. VERY FRESH TOFU
>1 CUP LIGHT MOLASSES
>  OR ¾ CUP LIGHT MOLASSES AND 2 TBS. HONEY
>½ CUP WATER
>3 TBS. CAROB POWDER
>¼ TSP. SALT
>½ TSP. VANILLA
>THE GELATIN MIXTURE

Whip in a large bowl until stiff
>½ PINT WHIPPING CREAM

Gently fold the blended ingredients into the whipped cream.
Turn into a pudding mold or 2 baked 9" pie shells.
Chill overnight.

# ORANGE CHIFFON MOLD

Soften
> 1 TBS. UNFLAVORED GELATIN

In
> ¼ CUP WATER

Heat to dissolve completely.

Mix in a blender until smooth
> 12 OZ. VERY FRESH TOFU
> 2 EGG YOLKS
> ¾ CUP HONEY
> ⅛ TSP. SALT
> THE GELATIN MIXTURE

Add and blend again
> 1 CAN (6 OZ.) FROZEN ORANGE JUICE
>    CONCENTRATE

Whip in a large bowl until stiff
> 2 EGG WHITES

Gently fold the blended ingredients into the egg whites.
Turn into a 4 cup mold.
Chill overnight.

# FAVORITE CRUMB CRUST

This is a very easy and delicious way to make use of dry bread.
Use the smaller amounts for an 8" pan, the larger for a 10" one.

Mix well in a medium bowl
       1 – 1½ CUPS VERY FINE DRIED BREAD CRUMBS
       4 – 6 TBS. DARK BROWN SUGAR
       4 – 6 TBS. MELTED BUTTER
       1 TSP. CINNAMON

Pat into an 8" or 10" spring form pan or pie pan.
Bake, if desired, at 325° for 15 minutes. Otherwise, chill until needed.

# APPLESAUCE TORTE

### THE CRUST (OPTIONAL)

Prepare **Favorite Crumb Crust** for a 10" spring form pan.
Reserve ¼ cup of the crumb mixture.
Put the remaining mixture into a 10" spring form pan.

### THE FILLING

Mix in a blender until smooth
　　　3 EGGS
　　　1 LB. VERY FRESH TOFU
　　　1 CUP HONEY
　　　¼ CUP WHOLEWHEAT FLOUR
　　　2 TBS. LEMON JUICE
　　　2 TBS. GRATED LEMON RIND
　　　1 TSP. CINNAMON
　　　¼ TSP NUTMEG
　　　1 TSP. VANILLA

Turn into a large mixing bowl.
Stir in
　　　2 CUPS UNSWEETENED APPLESAUCE

Pour into the crust.
Top with the reserved crumbs.
Bake at 350° for 1 hour.
Chill overnight.

# AVOCADO PIE

## THE CRUST

Prepare your favorite crumb crust for a 9" pie.
Bake if necessary.
Chill until needed.

## THE FILLING

Soften
> 1 TBS. UNFLAVORED GELATIN

In
> ⅛ CUP WATER

Heat to dissolve completely.

Mix in a blender until smooth
> 8 OZ. VERY FRESH TOFU
> 1 EGG
> ½ CUP HONEY
> ⅜ CUP FRESH LIME JUICE
> ⅛ TSP. SALT
> ⅛ TSP. FINELY GRATED LIME PEEL
> THE GELATIN MIXTURE

Add and blend again
> ½ MEDIUM AVOCADO

Turn into the prepared crust.
Garnish generously with
> CHOPPED WALNUTS

Chill thoroughly before serving.

# PEACHY PIE PHENOMENON

Prepare your favorite single 9" crust. (optional)

Mix in a medium-sized bowl
          2½ CUPS THINLY SLICED PEACHES
          ½ CUP UNSWEETENED COCONUT
          ¼ CUP HONEY
          2 TBS. WHOLEWHEAT FLOUR
          ½ TSP. CINNAMON
          ⅛ TSP. NUTMEG

Turn into the crust or a buttered 9" baking dish.
Dot with
          1 TBS. BUTTER (optional)

Mix in a blender until smooth
          2 EGGS
          12 OZ. VERY FRESH TOFU
          4 OZ. CREAM CHEESE
          ¾ CUP HONEY
          ½ TSP. CINNAMON
          ¼ TSP. SALT
          1½ TSP. VANILLA

Gently pour the blended ingredients over the peaches.
Do not stir.
Bake at 350° for 50 – 60 minutes.
Serve warm or chilled.

# CARROT PIE

## THE CRUST (OPTIONAL)

Prepare your favorite single 9" crust.
Bake at 400° for 5 minutes.

## THE FILLING

Mix in a blender until smooth
>       2 CUPS CHOPPED COOKED CARROTS
>       ¾ CUP HONEY
>       ¼ CUP LIGHT MOLASSES
>       1 EGG
>       1 TSP. VANILLA
>       ½ TSP. SALT
>       ½ TSP. GINGER
>       ½ TSP. CINNAMON
>       ¼ TSP. NUTMEG
>       ¼ TSP. ALLSPICE

Add and blend again
>       12 OZ. VERY FRESH TOFU

Add and mix gently with a long handled spoon
>       ¼ CUP RAISINS  (optional)

Turn into the pie shell or a lightly oiled 9" baking dish.
Bake at 350° for 50 – 60 minutes or until a knife inserted in the center comes out clean.
Chill thoroughly.

# YAM PIE

## THE CRUST (OPTIONAL)

Prepare your favorite single 9" crust.
Bake at 400° for 8 minutes.

## THE FILLING

Mix in a blender until smooth
    2 CUPS PURÉED COOKED YAMS
    1 LB. VERY FRESH TOFU
    1 CUP ORANGE JUICE
    ½ CUP BUTTER
    ½ CUP HONEY
    ¼ CUP LIGHT MOLASSES
    2 EGGS
    1½ TSP. GRATED LEMON RIND
    ½ TSP. SALT
    ¼ TSP. NUTMEG
    1 TSP. VANILLA

Turn into the pie shell or a lightly oiled 9" baking dish.
Bake at 350° for 35 – 40 minutes or until set.
Chill thoroughly.

# ALMOND CREME PIE

### THE CRUST (OPTIONAL)

Prepare your favorite single 10" pastry crust or crumb crust for a 10" spring form pan.
Bake as needed and cool completely.

### THE FILLING

Soak
>  2 TBS. UNFLAVORED GELATIN

In
>  ¼ CUP WATER

Heat to dissolve completely.
Mix in a blender until smooth
>  1 LB. VERY FRESH TOFU
>  1 CUP HONEY
>  3 EGG YOLKS
>  2 TSP. VANILLA
>  1½ TSP. ALMOND EXTRACT
>  ¼ TSP. SALT
>  THE GELATIN MIXTURE

In a medium-sized bowl beat stiff
>  3 EGG WHITES

In another bowl whip
>  1 CUP WHIPPING CREAM

Pour the tofu ingredients into a large bowl.
Gently fold both the egg whites and the whipped cream into the tofu ingredients.
Turn into the prepared crust or a pudding mold.

# PINEAPPLE ALMANDINE PIE

Prepare **Almond Creme Pie** (see facing page).
Chill overnight.
Cover with **Pineapple Topping** (see below).

## PINEAPPLE TOPPING

Drain well into a small sauce pan
> THE LIQUID FROM A 15 OZ. CAN OF JUICE-PACKED
> PINEAPPLE RINGS

Stir in
> 1 TBS. ARROWROOT OR CORNSTARCH
> ¼ CUP HONEY

Bring to a boil and cook, stirring constantly, until clear and thickened.
Remove from heat.
While the juice mixture is cooling slightly, arrange the pineapple rings on top of the Almond Creme Pie.
Pour the juice mixture gently over the rings.
Refrigerate until set.

# APPENDIX

# TOFU:
# A NUTRITIONAL PROFILE

8 OUNCES OF TOFU PROVIDE THE FOLLOWING: *

| | |
|---|---:|
| calories | 164.0 |
| protein | 17.6 g |
| fat | 9.6 g |
| carbohydrate | 5.4 g |
| calcium | 292.0 mg |
| phosphorus | 286.0 mg |
| iron | 4.4 mg |
| sodium | 16.0 mg |
| potassium | 96.0 mg |
| thiamine | 0.12 mg |
| riboflavin | 0.08 mg |

*Source: COMPOSITION OF FOODS, Agriculture Handbook No. 8, Agricultural Research Service, U.S. Dept. of Agriculture, 1963.

8 ounces of tofu provide the same amount of usable protein as *

    3¼ oz. steak . . . . . . . . . . at the cost of . . . . 230 calories
    5½ oz. hamburger . . . . . at the cost of . . . . 440 calories
    1⅔ cup milk . . . . . . . . . at the cost of . . . . 220 calories
    2 eggs . . . . . . . . . . . . . . . at the cost of . . . . 160 calories
    2 oz. cheese . . . . . . . . . at the cost of . . . . 200 calories


8 ounces of tofu provide about the same amount of calcium as **

    8 oz. of milk – Great for people who don't like or can't drink milk!


8 ounces of tofu provide about the same amount of iron as **

    4½ eggs . . . . . . . . . . . . . . at the cost of . . . . 360 calories
    2 oz. beef liver . . . . . . . . at the cost of . . . . . 80 calories


*Shurtleff, William, and Aoyagi, Akiko, THE BOOK OF TOFU, Autumn Press, U.S.A., 1975, page 25.

**Source: COMPOSITION OF FOODS, Agriculture Handbook No. 8, Agricultural Research Service, U.S. Dept. of Agriculture, 1963.

#  INDEX

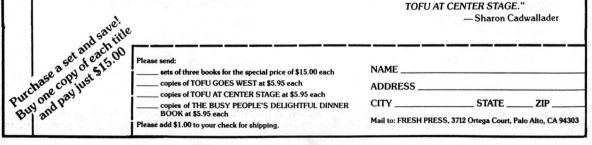